365 Tip $ for your financial life

# 365 Tip$ for your financial lif€

365 Tip $ for your financial life

Copyright © 2021 Cool & Co
All rights reserved
**ISBN: 9798771668857**
Independently published

# 365 Tip $ for your financial life

## Important information

This book has been written to provide educational information. Every effort has been made to make it as complete and accurate as possible. However, it gives information about internet marketing only up to the date of publication. Therefore, this book should be used as a guide - not as the definitive source of Internet marketing information.

Also in terms of finance, the world is constantly changing, so you should continue researching and updating your financial education.

The purpose of this book is to educate. The author and publisher do not guarantee that the information in this book is complete and will not be responsible for any errors or omissions. The author and publisher shall have no liability to any person or entity with respect to any loss or damage caused or allegedly caused by this book.

Remember that according to your situation and objectives you will apply the tips that you consider or adapt them as you consider. This will be your guide for you to continue your in-depth investigation.

365 Tip $ for your financial life

365 Tip $ for your financial life

## Table of Contents

Introduction .................................................. 6

365 Tips for Saving, Investing, and Making Money .......................................................... 8

Conclusion ................................................. 126

# 365 Tip $ for your financial life

## Introduction

When it comes to success in our professional and personal lives, few things are more important than achieving a reasonable standard of living through wise personal finance decisions. Through our job options, our savings, and our investment decisions, we determine what will be possible for us in the future, as well as when we can retire and how enjoyable our retirement will be.

In fact, all of this is very important. However, without the correct information available at our fingertips, we can often become paralyzed when it comes time to make those important decisions.

For example, when it comes time to save, we might decide to put it off for another day. Or when the time comes to invest, we could get ahead of ourselves and make the decision too soon, even with outstanding debt that carries high interest rates.

## 365 Tip $ for your financial life

In the rest of this book, we'll consider 365 different tips, one for each day of the year, that you can use to make these decisions the right way. Through this book, I hope that you not only learn how to be frugal, how to save, and how to invest, but also how to direct your career (and exploit money-making opportunities) in a way that brings you closer to financial security and a broader sense. satisfaction with your life and your choices.

# 365 Tip $ for your financial life

## 365 Tips to save, invest and earn money

**Tip # 1:** Buy products online.

A good way to limit impulse buying is to buy products online. It allows you to more easily compare stores, qualities, benefits and prices. And it will also save you from thinking you have to buy, so you don't have to travel to another place to do your shopping.

**Tip # 2:** Comparison search engines.

When making large purchases, you should always shop around. By spending an additional 20-30 minutes researching your options, you could easily save a lot of money.

**Tip # 3:** Use coupons.

Whether you're shopping for groceries or shopping for new electronics, using coupons is always a great way to save. So from now on, get in

# 365 Tip $ for your financial life

the habit of checking the newspaper and other local sources for coupons, as well as accumulation promotions and deals.

**Tip # 4:** Use coupon sites on the internet.

The internet is now flooded with online coupon sites. They collect and store coupons that can be printed and used at various physical stores. Before leaving your home, consider searching for coupons for your retail destination; and then put them to use.

**Tip # 5:** Enroll in rewards programs.

Grocery stores, clothing stores, and other retail stores now offer rewards programs. By signing up for a free membership, you can often get access to a variety of coupons, discounts, and cash back offers. Be sure to sign up for the rewards programs offered at all of your favorite stores.

**Tip # 6:** Look for special offers at the grocery store.

# 365 Tip $ for your financial life

Grocery stores often have specials on foods they suspect they won't be able to sell. Take advantage of these specials by buying food you want anyway, but at a steep discount.

**Tip # 7:** Create a shopping list in advance.

Eliminate junk food and nonessential foods by creating a shopping list in advance. At the end of the day, you will have spent less, and you will also have all the ingredients you will need for weekly meals.

**Tip # 8:** Wait for the sales.

Some stores have regular sales. For example, many stores have big discounts after Christmas and other major holidays to sell seasonal inventory. Take advantage of these predictable sales by delaying your purchases.

**Tip # 9:** Limit spending on entertainment.

Entertainment is important, but it can often be obtained cheaply. From now on, limit your entertainment spending until you've paid your

## 365 Tip $ for your financial life

monthly bills and saved a fixed portion of your income. It is not about not having leisure, if not about prioritizing, once the debts are paid, the basics for living and a percentage for savings.

**Tip # 10:** Reduce the amount of time you spend watching television.

Television can be an endless waste of time. It's easy to sit in front of the TV for hours on end, even if we have tasks that we could be working on to improve our lives and our finances. So try to reduce the amount of time you waste watching television.

**Tip # 11:** Avoid surfing the net aimlessly.

Similar to wasting time on television, surfing the internet is a bad habit that many of us have. Avoid doing it when there are other more productive things you could be doing.

**Tip # 12:** Get a sewing kit.

Get a sewing kit and learn how to use it. The next time your pants leg or shirt arm is ripped, just use the sewing kit to fix it, rather than buying a brand new item of clothing. It is not about wearing clothes full of patches, but sometimes we discard the same because of a ripped seam.

**Tip # 13:** Learn how to do basic home repairs.

Learning how to do basic home repairs can save you a lot of money. Instead of calling a plumber or carpenter, you can simply do the repairs yourself, saving you money. Obviously there will be certain types of repairs that you will require a professional for reasons of logistics, knowledge, etc., in this case do not hesitate, sometimes cheap is expensive. So be sure to pay someone to do it to your desired quality, and you don't have to repair again in no time.

**Tip # 14:** Limit spending on expensive toys.

As a parent, it is simply your natural inclination to do what you think is best for your child (and sometimes screw it up). But when it comes to toys, more (and more expensive) isn't always better. So before spending hundreds on the trendiest toys, think twice about whether your child could be better served by something less expensive.
I attach a decalogue of the toy for you to analyze:

## 365 Tip $ for your financial life

1. Choose games or toys where the child participates actively and is not just a simple spectator.

2. Find a game or toy that stimulates the child different aspects such as: creativity and imagination, socialization or cooperation, among others.

3. Think about the environment around us and try to choose products that are not made with materials that are harmful to health and the environment.

4. Remember the neighborhood store and local commerce: artisans often make games and toys with resistant and quality materials that last longer.

5. Check that the CE seal appears on the box where it says that the product has passed the quality controls.

6. There are many types of games and toys: board and board, traditional, construction, motor. We avoid warlike ones and those that reproduce gender stereotypes.

7. When wrapping the package, do it with paper that can be recycled later. In stores there are different types of paper but it must be remembered that those with shiny motifs and added plastic are harmful to the environment.

8. Be careful with advertising and read the fine print. Sometimes what you see in the media and what appears in the box that wraps the product is not really the same toy that it contains.

9. Think, with the game or toy in your hands, if the price you have indicated is appropriate. You do not have to keep a product if, truly, you are not convinced or convinced.

## 365 Tip $ for your financial life

10. *Sharing playtime with children is the best way to strengthen the emotional and educational bonds between parents and children. It should not be forgotten that fathers and mothers are the first playmates of the little ones.*

**Tip # 15:** Limit the cinema if you have debts.

Instead of going to the movies all the time, stay home and rent a movie through your cable TV service and get your own snacks. Instead of spending
€ 30-50, you will spend only € 10.

**Tip # 16:** Replace expensive foods with cheaper foods.

Instead of spending € 200 per week on groceries, think hard about which items are luxurious and which items are actually important components of your weekly menu. Ditch the expensive items in favor of the cheaper ones. From the unnecessary for the necessary.

**Tip # 17**: Buy private label products.

## 365 Tip $ for your financial life

White-label or generic products are cheaper and often identical to brand-name items. So instead of paying the premium for the brand name product immediately, consider at least trying the store brand once.

**Tip # 18:** Please use the slower shipping option.

When it comes to shopping online, it's often tempting to go for faster shipping. From now on, practice delayed gratification and go for the slower shipping option as long as there is a money difference in it.

**Tip # 19:** Buy gifts well in advance.

Many people wait until the last minute to buy gifts. As a result, they end up spending a lot of money the day or night before the event just to get something nice. Instead of doing this, allow yourself weeks or months to pick up the product. Instead of rushing in the night before, you might stumble upon him at a sale in the weeks leading up to the event.

**Tip # 20:** Make your own gifts.

# 365 Tip $ for your financial life

Candles, jewelry, mixing CDs, a home gymkhana... can often make excellent and highly personalized gifts. Instead of buying a gift at the store, consider making one for your friend or family member.

**Tip # 21:** Take public transportation.

Public transportation is often cheaper than owning, maintaining, and paying for gas for a car. Consider selling your car and making the switch.

**Tip # 22:** Walk more.

Instead of driving your car small distances to the store and the post office, consider walking to those places instead. Not only is it good for you, it will save you money on gas and wear and tear.

**Tip # 23:** Buy a speed pass for tolls.

If the region you live in offers an automatic toll pass, buy it. It may have a high upfront cost, but it will pay off in reduced tolls over time.

# 365 Tip $ for your financial life

**Tip # 24:** Buy a pass for public transport.

Buy a pass to take the local train or metro system. In the long run, you will save a lot of money by paying less each time you use public transport.

**Tip # 25:** Spend money on entertainment with a high reuse value.

Instead of wasting your money on video games and other forms of entertainment that cannot be reused, instead focus on forms of entertainment that have a high reuse factor. That is, try to get the most entertainment per dollar spent. Or cultural entertainment.

**Tip # 26:** Buy video games with high re-play value.

Similar to tip 25, buy video games that can be played 1,2,3, or more times. Don't settle for buying a $ 50 game that will no longer be pleasant after just one play.

**Tip # 27:** Limit carbonated beverages.

# 365 Tip $ for your financial life

Flavored, carbonated or carbonated beverages are expensive "luxury" that are often not worth the amount we pay, as well as being detrimental to our health. Instead, take a bottle of water with you and fill it at home using the tap.

**Tip # 28:** Make coffee or tea at home.

Buying coffee or tea at your favorite place can often be a pleasant experience. However, it is many times more expensive than making the same coffee or tea at home.

**Tip # 29:** Stop smoking.

Smoking is unhealthy and expensive, so quit smoking. Your body and pocket will appreciate it.

**Tip # 30:** Reduce the consumption of alcohol.

Excessive alcohol consumption is both unhealthy and unproductive. Reduce alcohol from your budget and your life. Your body and your pocket will continue to thank you.

# 365 Tip $ for your financial life

**Tip # 31:** Replace incandescent or fluorescent bulbs.

CFLs generate light without heat. For this reason, they use less energy. And now we have LEDs that are very low consumption.

**Tip # 32:** Use the air conditioner and / or heater less often.

Air conditioners and heaters can use a large amount of electricity. So if you don't need to keep a room warm or cool, don't use them. In summer, lower the blinds during hot and soft hours and open the windows at night to cool and ventilate the house.

**Tip # 33:** Make a market or sell in apps.

Running a flea market or selling through secondhand apps will help you get rid of the garbage that accumulates in your closets and collect some extra cash.

# 365 Tip $ for your financial life

**Tip # 34:** Spend more time comparing purchases for expensive products.

When it comes to high-cost items, spend more time comparative shopping. Consider using eBay, Google Shopping, and other online platforms to compare prices so that you get the best deal.

**Tip # 35:** Base plans of purchases and meals around the availability of coupons.

Instead of using a set menu to buy groceries, create your menu to fit coupon availability for a particular week. This will ensure that you save as much as possible every time you shop for groceries.

**Tip # 36:** Don't get addicted to spending.

Some of us "enjoy" just spending money. If you are one of those people, practice disciplining yourself by not throwing away cash simply when you feel depressed or bored.

**Tip # 37:** Meet with a financial planner.

# 365 Tip $ for your financial life

A financial planner can help you visualize your future; and how it will be shaped by today's savings decisions. Do this as soon as possible, and focus on a plan.

**Tip # 38:** Buy clothes at thrift stores.

Thrift stores often offer high-quality clothing for a mere fraction of the store price. Instead of spending all your money on expensive brands at retail stores, consider getting the same second-hand items.

**Tip # 39:** Buy from bulk stores.

Bulk stores allow you to get massive quantities of products at a steep discount. If you want to save money in the long run, shopping at these stores (and then stocking the remaining quantities of the item) is the way to go.

**Tip # 40:** Cook in bulk.

Cooking in bulk is another great way to save money and time. You can do this by producing a week's worth of food (or more) in a single cooking session. You can then freeze the remaining food and reheat it later in the week.

**Tip # 41:** Go on vacation less.

Vacations can be tremendously expensive, so try to reduce how often you take them. Sometimes less is more, and they can be replaced by alternative and much cheaper plans.

**Tip # 42:** Limit spending on vacations.

When you go on vacation, try to spend less. Instead of buying expensive hotel rooms, expensive dinners, and expensive drinks, try to enjoy the moments and focus on being happy, rather than achieving happiness through luxury.

**Tip # 43:** Go on a cheaper vacation.

Go camping or take a "bungalow". These can often be as fun as a vacation to a far away place, but a lot cheaper.

365 Tip $ for your financial life

**Tip # 44:** Refinance your home.

Since one of your biggest monthly expenses is probably your mortgage, it's always a good idea to consider whether or not you could benefit from refinancing. Do this periodically to confirm that you are receiving the best rate. Many people think that the mortgage is as it was signed for life. And interest rates go up and down constantly, so at the right time you can benefit from a good refinancing.

**Tip # 45:** Replace the steak with chicken and pork.

Steak is much more expensive than chicken and pork. Consider substituting it between meats to reduce the amount you spent on groceries.

**Tip # 46:** Eat less meat.

Relative to the nutritional value it provides, meat is one of the most expensive components of your grocery spend. Consider reducing the amount you consume. Also, watch out for the high intake of red meat.

## 365 Tip $ for your financial life

**Tip # 47:** Ask your credit card company to lower your interest rates.

Getting a lower interest rate on your credit card is often as simple as making a call to the company. Get in the habit of doing this on a regular basis.

**Tip # 48:** Pay off high-interest debt.

Instead of paying off low-interest debt, pay off high-interest debt. This will reduce the total amount you pay for debt service.

**Tip # 49:** Ask to be waived the fees.

Stores, credit card companies, and membership programs are often willing to waive fees if you claim that you will not use the service any other way.

**Tip # 50:** Ask your cable TV provider for a cheaper package.

# 365 Tip $ for your financial life

Instead of buying the most expensive cable bundle, consider downgrading to one that only contains the channels you need, but at a lower price.

**Tip # 51:** Move to a cheaper apartment or home.

If your rent or mortgage is unsustainably high, then move to a cheaper apartment or house.

**Tip # 52:** Re-finance your car.

Consider refinancing your car. If your income has increased or your credit has improved, you may be able to get a lower rate.

**Tip # 53:** Sell your car.

Cars are expensive. Consider selling yours and taking public transportation instead. Many times we have the car more on a whim than on necessity.

**Tip # 54:** Buy a cheaper car.

# 365 Tip $ for your financial life

Sell your car and buy a cheaper one, or maybe one that gets better gas mileage.

**Tip # 55:** Buy extra razor blades, instead of brand new razors.

Instead of buying a new razor, buy new blades, which are often now sold separately.

**Tip # 56:** Refill the ink cartridges, rather than buying new ones.

Ink cartridges can now generally be refilled using a tool kit and some toner. This is considerably less expensive than buying a new cartridge.

**Tip # 57:** Refinance your student or consumer loans.

If you are able to refinance your student or consumer loans at a lower rate, do so.

365 Tip $ for your financial life

**Tip # 58:** Create a carpool group to get to work.

You need to get to work; and so do your co-workers. Create a carpool group to save on gas and wear and tear.

**Tip # 59:** Improve your gas mileage.

Use tricks to improve gas mileage, like using cruise control. A few simple tricks could save you $ 20 or more each week.

**Tip # 60:** Add air to your car's tires.

Adding air to your car's tires (so they are properly inflated) can greatly improve your gas mileage.

**Tip # 61:** Try to fix broken items, rather than buying new ones.

Fixing broken chairs, railings, and other furniture or accessories in your home is cheaper than buying new ones.

# 365 Tip $ for your financial life

**Tip # 62:** Bring a bagged lunch to work.

If you're careful, you can bring bagged lunches to work for a week for the same price you'd spend on a single day if you had to go out for lunch.

**Tip # 63:** Limit how often you go out to dinner.

Dining out can be very expensive; And it's often easy to ignore exactly how expensive it is. Try to do it less often, just for special occasions.

**Tip # 64:** When you go to restaurants, buy cheaper dishes.

If you decide to go out to dinner, don't use it as a reason to splurge. Look for cheaper dishes and drink only water.

**Tip # 65:** Go to less expensive restaurants.

Not all restaurants are equally expensive. Instead of spending all your money on a fancy night, choose a cheaper one. It can easily be just as nice.

# 365 Tip $ for your financial life

**Tip # 66:** Shop at thrift stores.

Thrift stores typically carry a wide variety of secondhand items, including books, clothing, and furniture. Instead of buying new things, consider going to a thrift store first.

**Tip # 67:** Keep track of your debt.

Instead of just paying attention to your minimum payments, keep track of the total amount of debt you have, including student loans, credit card debt, and your mortgage.

**Tip # 68:** Keep a record of your savings and investments.

Many people make the mistake of ignoring their savings and investments. As a result, they make small profits, if at all. They also face the risk of large losses during recessions and bubble bursts. Pay attention to where you invest and save your money.

**Tip # 69:** Get term life insurance, rather than permanent.

Don't invest in life insurance. Instead, use it for its intended purpose - get term insurance.

**Tip # 70:** Use local exchange sites to find furniture.

Use local exchange sites for furniture. In many cases, you will be able to find bed frames, sofas, and shelves for free.

**Tip # 71:** Don't store your credit card numbers online on sites.

Storing your credit card information on sites like Amazon makes it easy for you to buy things you don't need, so don't. Make it more difficult by not saving your information.

**Tip # 72:** Avoid impulsive spending.

## 365 Tip $ for your financial life

Never buy in the heat of the moment. Instead, take some time to think about purchases, especially when they are large, before making the decision.

**Tip # 73:** Don't spend up to your credit limit.

Spending up to your credit limit is rarely a good idea. Instead, try to stay as far from your limit as possible.

**Tip # 74:** Call your credit card company regularly.

Your credit card company can do a lot for you. It can lower your APR, extend payment terms, and allow you to enter into an extended grace payment or debt settlement agreement. Take advantage of these services, rather than just skipping payments.

**Tip # 75:** Avoid carrying a positive balance on any card that has a positive interest rate.

If a credit card has a positive interest rate, you should cancel it immediately. Instead, transfer the balance to a card that temporarily has 0% APR or pay as soon as possible.

**Tip # 76:** Cut your credit card.

While closing credit card accounts can often look negative on credit reports, no one will know if you cut a card and throw it away. So cut off most of your credit cards and throw them away, but keep your bills.

**Tip # 77:** Use a credit card for small purchases.

To improve your credit, use your card for small everyday purchases. Pay the balance on these purchases each month.

**Tip # 78:** Please note the teaser rates.

Most credit card companies will offer an initial interest rate. Keep in mind that this is not your permanent APR, but a temporary APR that will likely change in a matter of months. This is also usually done by telephone companies, cable TV, etc. I take into account that for X time and then you go on to pay more.

# 365 Tip $ for your financial life

**Tip # 79:** Never exceed the credit limit on your card.

Exceeding your card's credit limit often carries costly penalties. Avoid doing it.

**Tip # 80:** Get a copy of your credit report.

At least twice a year, get a copy of your credit report to check for any errors or problems that have escaped you.

**Tip # 81:** Ask your bank for better conditions.

Call your bank and ask for better conditions. This could help you eliminate fees and get a higher interest rate on your bills or lower on your debts.

**Tip # 82:** Switch to a bank that has more ATMs in your area.

# 365 Tip $ for your financial life

If you are constantly paying fees to use other banks' ATMs, consider switching to a bank that offers more ATMs in your area.

**Tip # 83:** Put money in a certificate of deposit (CD).

CDs often require you to put money away for a set period of time (often 6 months or 12 months). This can be a useful device to avoid wasting money.

**Tip # 84:** Put a fixed fraction of your income in your savings.

Instead of thinking about how much to save each month, automatically put 10% of your income into savings each month. This is a good habit to develop earlier.

**Tip # 85:** Avoid investing the money you will need soon in stocks.

Stock returns can be volatile relative to other investment instruments; however, for this reason, investing in stocks tends to generate high returns in the long term. For this reason, do not invest the money you will need in the short term in stocks.

**Tip # 86:** If you plan to save money for retirement, put it in a mutual fund.

Put your retirement savings in a mutual fund. Talk to your advisor to make sure the money is well spent.

**Tip # 87:** Invest your money in index funds.

Index funds are often the cheapest to invest and provide one of the best risk-adjusted returns. Consider putting your retirement savings in index funds.

**Tip # 88:** Cut down on the extras on your mobile phone plan.

Ditch the extras on your cell phone plan, including extended data and text messaging plans.

# 365 Tip $ for your financial life

**Tip # 89:** Send text messages less often.

If you still use text messages and pay for it, text less often. But certainly if you have mobile data, install any free messaging application.

**Tip # 90:** Clean your car at home, instead of paying for it.

Instead of taking your car to the car wash, grab a bucket of soapy water and a large sponge and get to work. You could save a lot of money.

**Tip # 91:** Rotate your tires.

Rotating tires can significantly improve gas mileage and reduce wear. Make sure to do it regularly.

**Tip # 92:** Wash your car after snow storms.

If you live in a cold climate area, be sure to wash your car after snow storms to clean up all the salt. This will save you money on long-term maintenance costs.

# 365 Tip $ for your financial life

**Tip # 93:** Start biking.

Riding a bike is a great way to get in shape and save money. Do it instead of driving your car everywhere.

**Tip # 94:** Avoid clothing that requires expensive maintenance, such as dry cleaning.

Rather than opting for clothing that involves extensive dry cleaning, get clothing that requires no special care. This will save you a considerable amount of money on maintenance.

**Tip # 95:** Make your own cards to accompany the gifts.

Use one of the many sites available to create and print a personalized card. This is considerably cheaper than buying one from the store; and it can result in a more personalized card.

**Tip # 96:** Offer to babysit as a gift.

# 365 Tip $ for your financial life

If your friend or family member has children, offer to take care of them as a birthday present.

**Tip # 97:** Use open source software, rather than expensive proprietary software.

Open source software, like OpenOffice, is free. Consider downloading and using it, rather than using expensive software.

**Tip # 98:** Reduce your printing or print at the office.

Print less or print only when you can for free. This can save you a lot of money.

**Tip # 99:** Print unimportant documents in draft settings.

Cartridges can last much longer if they are primarily used to print draft-quality documents. From now on, consider using an eraser for documents that don't need to be high-quality.

365 Tip $ for your financial life

**Tip # 100:** Sell your old clothes on eBay, Vinted ...

If you have extra clothes that you no longer fit (or that you no longer like), sell them in any app for some extra money.

**Tip # 101:** Use eBay to sell old PCs and laptops or parts of them.

If you have an old computer that you no longer use, sell it on eBay or at least take apart and sell its parts, such as the processor, motherboard, and RAM.

**Tip # 102:** Use local apps or pages to sell old furniture.

Sell your old furniture on local exchange sites. Even if you don't make a lot of money on each piece, you can at least get someone to take your old furniture away for free.

**Tip # 103:** Negotiate the price of your car.

## 365 Tip $ for your financial life

Whenever you buy a car, negotiate the price, rather than accept what is offered. This can often save you several hundred euros.

**Tip # 104:** Bring someone who's good at bargaining next time you buy an expensive item.

If you are planning to buy an expensive item, such as a house or car or expensive jewelry, bring along a good bargainer or friend who is knowledgeable in the matter at hand. Make sure this person does the talking and helps you get a lower price.

**Tip # 105:** Avoid buying store warranties.

Store warranties for electronics and other products are often counterfeits. Given the likelihood of replacement, the cost of the warranty is simply too high.

**Tip # 106:** Look for independent product insurance online.

# 365 Tip $ for your financial life

If you buy an expensive cell phone or television, look for independent insurance online. This can often be obtained at a much lower price.

**Tip # 107:** Use a clothesline, instead of your dryer.

Consider using a clothesline instead of a dryer. It could save a lot of electricity.

**Tip # 108:** Turn off the lights when you are not using a room.

If you're not using a room, turn off the lights. Don't pay for electricity if you're not using it.

**Tip # 109:** Clean the coils in your refrigerator.

Cleaning your refrigerator coils regularly can significantly reduce the cost of refrigeration by improving its efficiency.

**Tip # 110:** Use a bank that offers online banking services.

## 365 Tip $ for your financial life

Being able to access your records online can make a big difference when it comes to saving and spending decisions, so use a bank that offers good online banking. Even today there is a difference between online banking, not just any is worth it.

**Tip # 111:** Pay your bills online.

Businesses are often willing to lower your bill if you pay online. Doing this for 3 to 5 businesses can reduce your bills by € 50 or more per month.

**Tip # 112:** Enroll in automatic bill pay.

Similar to tip 111, companies are also often willing to pay less if you sign up for automatic bill pay.

**Tip # 113:** Buy a coupon book to keep yourself entertained.

A coupon book is a book that contains hundreds of coupons for different products and events in your area. Consider paying the nominal fee of € 10 or € 20 to purchase one of these books.

## 365 Tip $ for your financial life

**Tip # 114:** Sign up for entertainment coupon sites.

Local coupon sites often offer region-specific coupons on a daily or weekly basis. Sign up for these sites to save on your entertainment and meal costs.

**Tip # 115:** Join a less expensive gym.

Gyms vary widely in price. Some cost only € 10 per month. Others cost more than € 100. Get out of your current gym and switch to a cheaper one that offers the amenities you need.

**Tip # 116:** Look for restaurant coupons.

Many sites, including restaurant.com, offer great coupons for dinners. By joining and taking advantage of these sites, you can eat for a fraction of the normal price.

That's for just € 2, you can get a € 20 meal.

# 365 Tip $ for your financial life

**Tip # 117:** Give up your gym membership and go for a run instead.

Instead of going to an expensive gym, give up your membership and stick to a regular jogging routine. In addition, in more and more parks there are machinery for bodybuilding and exercise.

**Tip # 118:** Go to morning movie screenings to save money.

Morning movie screenings typically cost ½ to 2/3 the price of night screenings. Consider changing movie viewing times to save money.

**Tip # 119:** Buy airline tickets well in advance.

In general, the more you buy airline tickets in advance, the cheaper they will be. So don't wait until the last minute. Also, consider buying it with your credit card if you accumulate points or cashback. Always having the money available for when the charge is passed to you.

**Tip # 120:** Do not accept quoted hotel prices. Instead, try to negotiate.

## 365 Tip $ for your financial life

Hotels are often willing to negotiate if you are willing to ask. So don't be silent unless you want to pay more.

**Tip # 121:** Bring snacks for the flights.

Instead of paying € 5, 10, 20 or more for snacks on flights, bring your own snacks and save some money.

**Tip # 122:** When traveling, consider staying in a hostel.

Whenever you travel, consider staying in a hostel, rather than a hotel. You can save up to € 80 per night if you are willing to stay in a common room and share a bathroom.

**Tip # 123:** Buy hygiene products in bulk online.

Buy hygiene products, such as toothpaste and mouthwash, online in bulk. This can save you a lot of money in the long run.

# 365 Tip $ for your financial life

**Tip # 124:** Buy makeup online and wholesale.

Similar to tip 123, save money by buying your makeup online in bulk.

**Tip # 125:** Avoid trends and fads.

Trendy and other trends and fashions can be expensive. Avoid them and focus on your long-term happiness.

**Tip # 126:** Have dental students do dental work for you.

Dental schools are often willing to do dental work for little money or at a discount. Consider doing work there instead of going to the dentist. There are also hair salons where trainees cut your hair for free.

**Tip # 127:** Get a medical checkup at a nearby college.

# 365 Tip $ for your financial life

Getting a checkup at a university, rather than a doctor, is often a good, low-cost alternative.

**Tip # 128:** Buy coupons on eBay.

Many people resell coupons that they have received on eBay. If you plan to shop at these stores, you can also purchase the coupons or gift cards to save money anyway.

**Tip # 129:** Housesit to get extra money.

One possible way to earn extra money is to take care of the house. This simply involves finding someone who needs a house sitter and then staying at their residence for a week or a month while on vacation.

**Tip # 130:** Offer to babysit for neighbors and family members.

If you want to earn money, a good way is to take care of the children of the neighbors or family members.

**Tip # 131:** Consider using online sites to find odd jobs.

Use sites like Craigslist, secondhand, fiverr... to find odd jobs. Depending on your skills, you will have a variety of different opportunities.

**Tip # 132:** Cook more often.

Save money by staying home and cooking more often instead of ordering food or going to restaurants.

**Tip # 133:** Use a high-yield savings account.

Instead of putting your money in a savings account with 0% yield, consider putting your money in a savings account with high yield. There are very few left due to the collapse of interest, so the best thing is some type of investment, but the emergency mattress you have is interesting that it is in such an account, since you will have it immediately.

**Tip # 134:** Link your checking and savings account.

## 365 Tip $ for your financial life

Linking your checking and savings accounts can help you avoid overdraft fees. Check if your bank offers this option.

**Tip # 135:** Avoid signing up for expensive bank account extras.

Rather than blindly accepting the expensive extras your bank offers, consider whether or not you need them.

**Tip # 136:** Pay for your car insurance in advance.

Consider paying for your auto insurance in advance to avoid the possibility of a late or unpaid payment.

**Tip # 137:** Make your car payments in advance.

Instead of making all your car payments on time, set a goal of paying them upfront and paying off your loan as soon as possible. If you have a flexible loan, this will reduce the amount of interest you pay in total.

# 365 Tip $ for your financial life

**Tip # 138:** Make an additional mortgage payment each year.

Paying your mortgage sooner rather than later can save you a considerable amount on interest payments.

**Tip # 139:** Avoid credit cards with annual fees.

Don't get credit cards that have annual fees. Instead, only look for cards that are free to hold and use, as long as you pay the balance in full.

**Tip # 140:** Don't get rental car insurance.

Rental car insurance is often not worth it. Instead, just use your own insurance.

**Tip # 141:** Don't buy lottery tickets.

The expected return on a lottery ticket is negative. Don't buy them.

## 365 Tip $ for your financial life

**Tip # 142:** Do not play poker or gamble in any discipline.

Unless you have a lot of money to waste, opt out of poker games unless the stakes are very low. In addition, gambling or casinos end up creating addiction.

**Tip # 143:** Don't go to the casinos.

Casinos would not be able to operate if their expected returns were negative. For this reason, every time you go to a casino, you should expect to lose money.

**Tip # 144:** Try to find free or inexpensive parking, rather than settling for an expensive garage.

If you're going somewhere, try to find free or inexpensive street parking, rather than opting for expensive garage parking.

**Tip # 145:** Perform routine maintenance on your car.

# 365 Tip $ for your financial life

You should always perform routine maintenance on your car, rather than waiting for something to go wrong.

**Tip # 146:** Always shop around for insurance.

Instead of taking the first quote you get, shop around for auto insurance and other types of insurance.

**Tip # 147:** Talk to a financial planner about the best way to invest your money.

Instead of investing your money without planning first, start by talking to a financial planner. It could save you a lot of trouble and hassle in the long run.

**Tip # 148:** Install and use Skype or similar.

For long distance phone calls, use Skype, instead of your phone. You can save hundreds of dollars by making frequent long distance calls.

# 365 Tip $ for your financial life

**Tip # 149:** Rent console video games.

Instead of paying € 50 for a new console game, rent it for € 5. Since you will likely only play it once completely, this will save you money.

**Tip # 150:** Use a thermostat that can be programmed.

A programmed thermostat can ensure that your heating only turns on when it's cold and turns off when it's too hot. This will help prevent wasted energy.

**Tip # 151:** Waterproof your home.

By waterproofing your home, you can significantly lower your heating and cooling costs in the long run.

**Tip # 152:** Plant trees and shrubs strategically to save on energy costs.

# 365 Tip $ for your financial life

A few strategically placed trees and shrubs can go a long way in keeping your home out of the wind and shaded from sunlight.

**Tip # 153:** Buy used things when possible.

Whenever possible, buy used books, used clothing, and used furniture. You will save a lot of money.

**Tip # 154:** Repair your car when possible.

When feasible and safe, make minor repairs to your car yourself. For example, if you have a scratch, go to your local auto parts store and buy the correct color spray paint to do the repair job yourself.

**Tip # 155:** Paint the rooms in your house yourself.

Doing a good paint job inside your home doesn't have to be difficult. Next time you need it, please do it on your own terms.

# 365 Tip $ for your financial life

**Tip # 156:** Make the repairs to your house yourself.

Get in the habit of doing home repairs yourself. Try to fix broken faucets, light fixtures, and other items yourself, without paying for outside help.

**Tip # 157:** Buy gifts after the holidays.

Instead of sending gifts on time, buy them on sale after the holiday season and then send them off.

**Tip # 158:** Buy used textbooks at half.com.

Use sites like half.com to buy used textbooks at a great discount (if you're a student).

**Tip # 159:** Look for furniture and items on the sidewalks.

Many people leave discarded furniture and other items by the curb. Consider scanning curbs for items that can be a nice addition to your home. Cleaning and customizing them is a nice job, saves money and nothing better than custom furniture.

# 365 Tip $ for your financial life

**Tip # 160:** Avoid paying for delivery. Instead, pick up the food.

Delivery is an expensive luxury. Unless absolutely necessary, pick up your food instead.

**Tip # 161:** Cut back on perishable food.

Instead of buying perishable foods, buy foods that last longer. Buy the fresh ones within a few days to prevent them from deteriorating or over-ripening and we end up throwing them away.

**Tip # 162:** Buy canned goods and other items that last longer.

Canned food will last significantly longer than fresh food. Consider swapping most items for canned food to make sure the food will last when you don't eat it right away.

# 365 Tip $ for your financial life

**Tip # 163:** Periodically reassess the wastefulness of your purchases.

Instead of continuing with your useless ways, take the time to re-evaluate whether your expenses are useless or not; and adjust your expenses accordingly.

**Tip # 164:** Don't max out on pre-granted loans.

Instead of getting the most out of a loan simply by having it available to us, get what is just and necessary. Even in the case of "good" debt to be able to repay it as soon as possible.

**Tip # 165:** Don't apply for a loan simply because you qualify for it.

Just because you qualify for a loan doesn't mean it's always a good idea to take it. Think carefully before taking one out.

**Tip # 166:** Don't just take a loan from the dealer when you buy a car.

# 365 Tip $ for your financial life

Whenever you buy a car, the dealer will try to offer you financing. Instead of taking this simply because it's there, try to get a better rate from an external option.

**Tip # 167:** Compare all the loans you can get with the loans that e-loan.com offers you.

When it comes to obtaining a loan, always compare what you are offered with what you can get with an electronic loan.

**Tip # 168:** Pay your bills on time to avoid late fees.

Never miss an invoice payment. It may not seem like a big deal one day, but in reality, it can translate into tarnished credit and expensive fees.

**Tip # 169:** Tutor students at your local high school to earn money.

If you need to earn money, consider tutoring students at a school in your area. Focus on an area in which you have expertise.

365 Tip $ for your financial life

**Tip # 170:** Pick a summer job, as a lifeguard.

Choose a summer or field job. In addition to your normal job, it will help you earn some extra money.

**Tip # 171:** Choose a winter job, like gift wrapping.

Winter jobs and seasonal jobs can also be a nice addition to your normal job.

**Tip # 172:** Add a part-time job to your full-time job.

If you are already working full-time, consider choosing a part-time job to increase your income. Obviously as a temporary measure to get out of debt. It is not the idea to live working all our time.

**Tip # 173:** Meet with a professional counselor.

Don't just think in the short term. Consider how you can improve your long-term income prospects by talking to a professional counselor and getting organized.

**Tip # 174:** Go back to school to improve your career prospects.

Going back to school is one of the best ways to get ahead in life. If you are currently stuck in a dead-end job, consider going back to school for an MBA or another practical degree. There is no better investment than in educating yourself.

**Tip # 175:** Periodically apply for new jobs to see what types of offers you can get.

If you're wondering what kind of salary the market could offer you, the best way to find out is to apply. Do this regularly to see if your prospects for promotion are good or not.

**Tip # 176:** Blog on a topic that interests you and use AdSense to generate income.

Pick a niche. Blog about that niche. And then you add ads to your blog to generate ad revenue.

# 365 Tip $ for your financial life

**Tip # 177:** Sell ClickBank products as an affiliate.

Pick a niche and sell ClickBank products in that niche. You can do this by using AdWords or by publishing them on an existing site.

**Tip # 178:** Create digital products and sell them with PayPal.

Create digital products, such as short e-books or audio content. Next, set up a small site, drive traffic to it, and accept payment through PayPal.

**Tip # 179:** Start your own physical business.

Start your own physical business. Put it in your home originally, but then move to a retail store once things get a chance to grow.

**Tip # 180:** Make improvements to your current business.

## 365 Tip $ for your financial life

If you have an existing business, consider making improvements to help reduce costs in the long run or improve your scope.

**Tip # 181:** Reduce the costs incurred by your current business.

Another way to earn more money is to cut costs in your current business. Find ways to do things more efficiently and lower your input costs.

Tip # 182: Get a roommate.

If you want to spend less on rent, get a roommate.

**Tip # 183:** Add an extra roommate.

If you already have a roommate, but still have a spare room, consider adding another roommate to further reduce costs.

## 365 Tip $ for your financial life

**Tip # 184:** Go find another apartment to find a better deal.

If your current apartment is too expensive, spend more time searching for your next apartment so that you can get a better price for the amenities you get.

**Tip # 185:** Ask for discounts on insurance, such as good student discounts.

Many insurance companies offer discounts for students and for other reasons. Where applicable, be sure to get these discounts.

**Tip # 186:** Move into a house with fewer (or no) unused rooms.

If you live in a home with many extra rooms, consider moving to one with fewer or no empty rooms to cut down on unnecessary mortgage and heating costs.

**Tip # 187:** Get an energy audit.

# 365 Tip $ for your financial life

An energy audit can help you determine where you are wasting energy, so you can adjust your behavior and save costs.

**Tip # 188:** Try to minimize utility costs.

Whenever possible, reduce utility costs by reducing energy and water use.

**Tip # 189:** Take advantage of free financial counseling services.

Many nonprofit organizations offer free financial counseling services. Take advantage of these if possible.

**Tip # 190:** Go to the student aid office for advice on your loans.

If you are a student, go to the financial aid office for advice on your loans. Find out which types of loans are best for your particular situation. As well as the scholarships available.

# 365 Tip $ for your financial life

**Tip # 191:** Take advantage of local libraries.

Instead of buying books, videos, and CDs, borrow them from your local library.

**Tip # 192:** Take advantage of the parks.

Going to a park is a good alternative to the more expensive forms of entertainment.

**Tip # 193:** Follow your favorite stores on Facebook to get coupons.

Many stores now have Facebook pages that they use to advertise deals. Join the pages of the stores you stop at most often.

**Tip # 194:** Sign up for newsletters online to offer free coupons to subscribers.

Many online newsletters offer coupons for their own and other products for free. Join these newsletters and take advantage of the offers.

**Tip # 195:** Use the same service for Internet, cable TV and telephone.

Using the same service for the Internet, cable TV, and telephone can save you a lot of money.

**Tip # 196:** Put all your accounts together in a financial app.

These applications record all your expenses and income and send you reports of your financial health as well as your financial score.

**Tip # 197:** Send for refunds.

When you buy a product that comes with a refund, send it back.

**Tip # 198:** Get refurbished electronic devices, such as cell phones or laptops.

Instead of paying full price for new electronics, buy refurbished electronics to save money.

# 365 Tip $ for your financial life

**Tip # 199:** Use recommended energy-saving appliances.

When furnishing your kitchen and other rooms with appliances, consider purchasing only government agency approved energy efficient appliances to save on your utilities in the long run.

**Tip # 200:** Buy generic over-the-counter drugs, rather than buying the brand-name versions.

When buying over-the-counter drugs, get generic versions, rather than brand-name ones. They are chemically identical, but cheaper.

**Tip # 201:** Take advantage of employer pension and investment matching programs.

Many companies offer pension plans, company shares, or other investment contributions. Take advantage of these programs by putting a larger portion of your income directly into your investment account.

# 365 Tip $ for your financial life

**Tip # 202:** Increase your insurance deductible.

Increasing your auto insurance deductible will significantly lower the premium you pay each month.

**Tip # 203:** Don't always file insurance claims.

Before filing an insurance claim, decide whether or not it's worth it. For example, will the $ 500 you avoid paying out of pocket be less than the amount you will pay in higher premiums?

**Tip # 204:** Apply for credit cards with 0% interest.

Whenever possible, get a 0% APR credit card and transfer your high-interest credit card debt to that card.

**Tip # 205:** Eliminate costly sources of debt.

Not all sources of debt are the same. Eliminate those that incur massive financing expenses by paying them first or taking out a consolidation loan to eliminate them.

365 Tip $ for your financial life

**Tip # 206:** Go to a health fair for low cost services.

Health fairs often offer deeply discounted rates on physicals, blood pressure checks, and other routine medical procedures. Take advantage of these to save some money.

**Tip # 207:** Do not go to the emergency room or use other high-cost medical services.

Instead of going to the emergency room, make an appointment with a doctor. The anticipation of check-ups will save you expenses in private urgent check-ups.

**Tip # 208:** Use a medical test kit for routine procedures.

In many cases, using a healthcare kit can be an inexpensive alternative to visiting a doctor. See what tests are available for your situation; and decide if it's worth it or not.

**Tip # 209:** Look for free health care services.

Next time you see a free health clinic or some other free health care service, take advantage of it.

**Tip # 210:** Argue the insurance claims against you.

The next time you are involved in a car accident, work hard to make your case. Don't just let the insurance companies listen to the other person's side of the story.

**Tip # 211:** Make sure you present your case clearly and in detail to the insurance companies.

Call your insurance company and work with the person involved in your claim. Make sure you don't get bogged down with fraudulent claims that are unrelated to your accident.

**Tip # 212:** Buy new glasses whenever deals are available.

From time to time, companies will offer big discounts on glasses. Whenever they are available, take advantage of them to get a new pair of glasses.

**Tip # 213:** Whiten your teeth at home with store-bought products, rather than paying for professional services.

Instead of paying for professional teeth whitening services, shop at a convenience store and use it at home. This can save you hundreds of dollars and produce comparable results.

**Tip # 214:** Use the euro stores.

While much of the euro store inventory is frivolous items, some things are really useful. Look for these items and save.

**Tip # 215:** For home-cooked meals, avoid pre-cut foods and chop foods at home.

Buying food before you cut it will save you a great deal of money. Get in the habit of doing this.

# 365 Tip $ for your financial life

**Tip # 216:** Pay attention to receipts.

When at the cash register, pay attention to the price of each item as it is entered. Also, check your receipt after you are done to make sure you have been charged correctly for each item.

**Tip # 217:** Complain if the price of the scanned item does not match the price on the shelf.

In some cases, the prices will not have been updated in the store system; and as a result, the scanner will not get a discount. Make sure to request the discount in these cases.

**Tip # 218:** make money buying and reselling on eBay or other platforms.

Look at the basket of bargains in clothing stores and other outlets. Get items on sale and then sell them online.

**Tip # 219:** Set up an eBay store.

# 365 Tip $ for your financial life

One way to earn a reputation on eBay and speed up your sales is to create a store. Do this to sell your bargain box merchandise.

**Tip # 220:** Buy products at government auctions and sell them on eBay.

If you want to make money without making a large investment, consider purchasing products at a deep discount at government auctions; and then resell them on eBay.

**Tip # 221:** Use inexpensive methods to promote your business, such as online advertising.

Instead of using expensive promotional methods, try using targeted advertising for your traditional business, such as online contextual ads.

**Tip # 222:** Advertise your business or services through brochures and apps.

Advertise your physical business or your services through brochures and apps.

## 365 Tip $ for your financial life

**Tip # 223:** Locate the junk and sell it at a junkyard.

Junkyards are often willing to pay hundreds of dollars for large pieces of aluminum or other metals. Consider using sites like Craigslist to locate scrap pieces so that you can collect and resell them.

**Tip # 224:** Offer to drive co-workers and friends to common places if they are willing to cover part of the gas.

Whenever possible, try to organize a carpool with your friends and co-workers. This will allow them to share in the cost of gas and wear and tear on the car.

**Tip # 225:** Create and sell content online.

If you're good at writing, consider writing articles, e-books, or reports and then selling them online.

**Tip # 226:** Work through Elance.com as a consultant.

If you want to make money online, consider working as a consultant in your area of expertise at Elance.com.

**Tip # 227:** Find freelance writing projects online.

Find freelance projects on Elance.com, feverr, and other sites to earn money in your spare time.

**Tip # 228:** Choose autonomous programming projects online.

Use sites like rentacoder.com to do additional programming work to earn more money in your spare time.

**Tip # 229:** Offer to sell your friends and neighbors' stuff on eBay for a small commission.

Do you know someone who has some extra junk lying around in their house? Offer to sell it online on eBay for a small commission.

**Tip # 230:** Create a CafePress store and sell T-shirts or other products.

CafePress allows you to create your own products, such as mugs, t-shirts, and bumper stickers. If you are a creative person, create your own store and then use it to sell your personalized merchandise.

**Tip # 231:** Sell affiliate products using Commission Junction.

Sell electronic and tangible products as an affiliate using sites like Commission Junction.

**Tip # 232:** Use Linkshare.com to sell tangible products as an affiliate.

Some of the largest and most respected corporations sell their products through independent affiliates at linkshare.com. Consider creating an account and selling your products through your existing website (or creating a new website to do so).

**Tip # 233:** Sell individual stock photos.

## 365 Tip $ for your financial life

Take pictures of everyday things, such as sunsets, sunrises, buildings, animals, and nature scenes. Sell these individual photos on a stock photo site.

**Tip # 234:** Sell stock photo light boxes.

If you are a good photographer, create a photo lightbox for a particular subject and then sell it on a stock photo site.

**Tip # 235:** He works as a blogger for a salary.

Using Elance.com or another site, find a site administrator who needs a full-time blogger. If you are a good writer who can create smart blog posts, this is a good way to make money.

**Tip # 236:** Sell support services for open source software.

Since anyone can do it legally, consider providing paid support for open source software, such as OpenOffice or WordPress. Use forums to market your services.

## 365 Tip $ for your financial life

**Tip # 237:** Sell WordPress templates.

If you are a reasonably good programmer with an eye for design, consider creating and selling WordPress templates. Good templates can fetch around $ 25 a piece.

**Tip # 238:** Offer remote software helpdesks.

If you are a tech savvy, market your services through Elance.com as a remote software installer or troubleshooter. Services like these can cost up to € 40 an hour.

**Tip # 239:** Buy and sell websites.

Using sitepoint.com and other online site marketplaces, buy, develop, and resell sites. If you are good at it, this can be a great way to make money.

**Tip # 240:** Invest in "virtual real estate".

## 365 Tip $ for your financial life

Instead of investing all your savings in stocks and bonds, put some of them on domains, fully developed sites, or other forms of virtual real estate.

**Tip # 241:** Sell banner ads on your website.

If you have a site that generates traffic, consider selling banner ad space to generate income.

**Tip # 242:** Sell cost-per-click (CPC) ads on your site through Google AdSense.

Instead of selling banner ads, consider selling CPC advertising through Google AdSense on your site.

**Tip # 243:** Sell CPC ads on your site using YPN.

Consider using YPN, rather than AdWords, to generate income for your site.

**Tip # 244:** Use PayPerPost and review products on your blog for money.

# 365 Tip $ for your financial life

If you have a popular blog, consider using PayPerPost, which will pay you to review products on your blog.

**Tip # 245:** Develop and sell sites.

Instead of buying, developing, and selling sites, start with the development phase. Pick a niche, develop a viable site, promote it, and then sell it.

**Tip # 246:** Create a network of sites to earn money.

Instead of creating a single site and reselling it, create a network of sites that complement each other. For example, you can create a specialized social networking site to generate traffic; And then you could funnel that traffic to a retail site.

**Tip # 247:** Create your own forum.

Pick a niche, create a forum, and then create that forum. Once you have accumulated a large

## 365 Tip $ for your financial life

number of members, sell it on sitepoint.com or another site marketplace.

**Tip # 248:** Buy and grow a forum.

Instead of developing your own forum, buy someone else's forum, improve it, send traffic to it, and then sell it again.

**Tip # 249:** Sell your services on Sitepoint.com.

In addition to selling your services on Elance.com and Guru.com, sell your services elsewhere, such as sitepoint.com.

**Tip # 250:** Find a talented warriorforum.com member to apprentice.

If you are looking to develop long-term entrepreneurial skills, consider working as an apprentice (free) for an entrepreneur from warriorforum.com or another popular marketing or business forum.

**Tip # 251:** Create an e-book and sell it.

If you are an expert on a topic and a good writer, create an e-book and sell it online for a relatively inexpensive price.

**Tip # 252:** Create a report and give it away for free.

If you have an existing site, create a short PDF report and give it away for free. Within the report, include links pointing to your site, so that everyone who reads the report is exposed to your site.

**Tip # 253:** Sell a hardcover book.

If you already have an ebook that is selling well, consider converting it to a hardcover book through a desktop publishing site; and then resell it.

**Tip # 254:** Create and give away video content to promote your site.

365 Tip $ for your financial life

In addition to giving away free reports, also consider giving away video content. You can do it using Camtasia or Camstudio.

**Tip # 255:** Create and give away audio content to promote your site.

Use free software to create audio content. Use this audio content to promote your existing website for more sales.

**Tip # 256:** Create an email list.

Regardless of whether you own a website or not, consider creating an email list; and then market products and services to that list.

**Tip # 257:** Send messages to your email list.

If you have an email list, sell products affiliated with your list for a commission or create new products to sell to you.

**Tip # 258:** Sell ads on your email list.

In addition to launching affiliate products and your own products to email lists, consider allowing other business owners to pay to advertise on your email list. If you have a large list, this can be quite profitable.

**Tip # 259:** Arbitrate on eBay and other auction sites.

Use eBay to find unusually cheap products. Resell those same products on eBay or other auction sites for a higher price.

**Tip # 260:** Work as a copywriter for an internet marketer.

Find an internet marketer in need of a copywriter at warriorforum.com. Offer to do the writing work at a big discount.

**Tip # 261:** Sell your copywriting skills on Elance.com.

## 365 Tip $ for your financial life

In addition to selling your skills to the marketers at the Warrior Forum, consider selling your copywriting services on Elance.com as well.

**Tip # 262:** Work as a freelance pet sitter for families in your area.

Find families in your area who need a pet sitter. Offer to take the job.

**Tip # 263:** Sell professional dog walking services.

Consider selling dog walking services to families in your area. This can be very profitable, especially if you can walk multiple dogs at the same time.

**Tip # 264:** Do freelance yard work, like mowing the lawn.

Take odd jobs as a landscaper. Volunteer to mow, mow, and remove weeds.

**Tip # 265:** Shovel or plow driveways.

## 365 Tip $ for your financial life

In the winter, offer to shovel or plow driveways. This will work especially well if you have a plow and truck, as you can easily earn $ 20 plowing a short driveway.

**Tip # 266:** Get a part-time job in a store and take advantage of the discount.

Department stores often offer deep discounts to employees. Get a job in one of them and take advantage of the discount to buy everything cheaper.

**Tip # 267:** Work as a caddy on a golf course.

While working as a caddy may seem like a menial job, you can often build good connections in the process. Consider doing it at your local golf course. It can also be a prop in any sports club.

**Tip # 268:** Look for joint venture partners.

If you have a business or a product, look for joint venture partners to promote your business,

## 365 Tip $ for your financial life

franchise it, or expand it along some profitable dimension.

**Tip # 269:** Save 10% of your income.

If you want to save money, commit to putting in at least 10% of your income initially. Over time, consider increasing this amount.

**Tip # 270:** Put your saved money in long-term investments, so you can't withdraw it.

If you're having trouble avoiding spending money, use investment accounts that incur fees if you withdraw money early. This will give you an incentive not to cheat.

**Tip # 271:** Set up money to be automatically withdrawn from your bank account and placed in a mutual fund or investment account.

To make saving easier, set up your bank account so that money is automatically sent to an investment account after your paycheck is deposited.

**Tip # 272:** Do not carry cash.

Having cash on hand will make you more likely to spend it. Instead, try to carry very little cash.

**Tip # 273:** Set goals and stick to them.

When it comes to saving, setting goals is vital. Decide where you want to go, commit to it, and then do it.

**Tip # 274:** Buy books and clothing at thrift stores and sell them online.

Go to thrift stores where second-hand furniture and clothing are sold. Buy them at a big discount and then sell them on sites like eBay and Amazon.

**Tip # 275:** Provide proofreading services for students.

If you are a good writer, consider offering proofreading services for college students for a nominal fee. You can do this at a local university or by searching for students on sites like Elance.com.

**Tip # 276: Work like a paid forum poster.**

If you already like posting on forums, consider accepting a job as a forum poster. Typically, you will be assigned to a niche and a set of forums; and then you will have to meet a certain quota of forum posts each day.

**Tip # 277:** Become a paid site administrator.

If you have good site management and programming skills, consider becoming a site administrator for various small Internet-based businesses. You can find these jobs through freelance sites and forums.

**Tip # 278:** Schedule a useful script and sell it.

If you have programming skills, create a useful script and sell it on a hungry market, such as a related forum.

**Tip # 279:** Hire a programmer to develop a script and resell it.

If you don't have any programming skills, hire a developer to create the script for you. And then market it and sell it yourself.

**Tip # 280:** Develop a Facebook application.

If you have an interest in developing apps, consider developing one for a massive platform, like Facebook.

**Tip # 281:** Sell script installation services.

If you don't have development skills, but can install site scripts, offer that service for a low fee on business forums and on Elance.com.

**Tip # 282:** Make paid directory submissions.

Offer to submit sites to link directories for a fixed price. Do this on webmaster forums and on freelance sites.

**Tip # 283:** He works as an SEO consultant.

If you have experience promoting sites, consider working as a freelance SEO consultant. While this may not be a full-time job, it may not be a bad way to earn additional income.

**Tip # 284:** Work on independent data entry.

Data entry is a simple job that does not generally require high-level skills. Consider looking for data entry jobs on Elance.com for when you have free time.

**Tip # 285:** Rent a server and let people buy storage space.

To earn some extra money, consider renting a server and then using that server to sell storage space to people who own and run Internet-based businesses.

## 365 Tip $ for your financial life

**Tip # 286:** Work as a domain name speculator.

Buying, maintaining, and reselling domains can be very profitable if you do it right. Consider working as a domain name speculator to earn some extra money.

**Tip # 287:** Create a subscription site in a niche that interests you.

If you have a keen interest in a particular niche, consider creating an online subscription site that provides information, software, and books related to that topic.

**Tip # 288:** Design and sell site logos.

If you have a knack for website design, consider designing and selling webmaster logos on sites like sitepoint.com.

**Tip # 289:** Sell clip art.

Similar to tip 288, but with clip art.

**Tip # 290:** Sell custom avatars for forums.

Similar to tip 288, but with forum avatars.

**Tip # 291:** Inter-site middleman link exchanges for a fee.

To generate traffic, sites need to get inbound links from high traffic and public relations sites. Consider working to negotiate exchanges and sales between sites that want to acquire links from high PR sites.

**Tip # 292:** Eliminate credit card debt before investing.

When it comes to investing, try to eliminate all your credit card debt before investing money. Since the interest rate on your credit cards is higher than your yield, the best investment you can make is to eliminate it.

# 365 Tip $ for your financial life

**Tip # 293:** Eliminate debt in order of the size of the interest rate.

When you eliminate credit card debt, do it in order of the size of the interest rate. The highest interest rates must come first.

**Tip # 294:** Take a moderate amount of risk when investing.

Whenever you invest, take at least a little risk. Otherwise, you are unlikely to get a return greater than 0%. Life is a risk, each one simply minimizes them as far as they are willing to bear.

**Tip # 295:** Don't put all your money in bonds.

As with tip 294, don't approach investing too conservatively, especially if you're investing for a distant retirement.

**Tip # 296:** Stop increasing your consumption when your income increases.

365 Tip $ for your financial life

When your income increases, add more to your income, rather than your consumption. It is an ideal occasion to establish or readjust your financial plan, do not let it escape.

**Tip # 297:** Practice frugality in all your choices.

In all the decisions in your life, practice frugality. Try to find a cheap, but good enough option, rather than the more expensive option. Read the "Desot Method" and put it into practice.

**Tip # 298:** Don't try to "keep up" with your friends.

Stop trying to "keep up" with your friends by spending more. Instead, accept that the newer, bigger TV and a new car may simply be out of your financial reach. And nothing happens.

**Tip # 299:** Live simply.

Practice living simply and enjoying simple, inexpensive activities. Don't rely on money to bring happiness. Enjoy the moments, not the things. Maximum of minimalism.

**Tip # 300:** Create a budget and follow it carefully.

Rather than letting ad-hoc expenses rule your life, create a monthly budget and follow it carefully. Unless you have a very good reason, don't deviate.

**Tip # 301:** Make a budget with your spouse.

If you are married or living with a partner, make a joint budget with your spouse. Instead of exchanging money with each other, find out how much you have together and determine your financial decisions together.

**Tip # 302:** Update your budget at least once a month.

At least once a month, reconsider the budget you have created and decide if you have allocated the correct amounts to the correct categories. If it's unrealistic or puts too much in a particular category, readjust your budget.

365 Tip $ for your financial life

**Tip # 303:** Use the lowest octane fuel allowed for your car by the owner's manual.

If your car doesn't require high-octane fuel, don't use it. It does nothing to help your car and is more expensive.

**Tip # 304:** Look for cheaper renters or home insurance.

Don't just pick the first option you have for renters or homeowners insurance. Instead, try to find a company that offers the right kind of coverage and at a price you can afford.

**Tip # 305:** Avoid taking out home equity loans.

Home equity loans are a good way to make sure you never pay your mortgage and never own your home. Unless you need to buy one to cover medical bills or something equally important, don't get it.

**Tip # 306:** Look periodically for a refinance.

## 365 Tip $ for your financial life

Every once in a while, look around to refinance your mortgage. You could save a huge amount on monthly payments by lowering your interest rate a little.

**Tip # 307:** Adjust your withholding tax to get a raise.

In many cases, your withholding will be too high. Take the time to adjust it, so you can have the money now, instead of when you pay taxes.

**Tip # 308:** Switch to paperless notifications for your invoices.

Many companies will take between € 5 and € 10 off your bill when you use electronic notifications exclusively. Do this with all your bills.

**Tip # 309:** Use the library instead of buying new books.

Instead of buying new books, use your local library or college library to check out the book.

365 Tip $ for your financial life

**Tip # 310:** Look for DVDs in the library, rather than renting them.

Use your local library to borrow DVDs, instead of paying € 5-10 to rent them for a few days.

**Tip # 311:** Sell your car and use an e-carpooling service to get to work.

Use an e-carpooling service to find a ride to work. You can usually do this without owning a car, as long as you are willing to pay for gas.

**Tip # 312:** Check if your checking and / or fund account is insured by the government.

If the government insures your account, you will not risk losing money if something happens to the bank, which you are using to save.

**Tip # 313:** Look for the savings account that offers the highest return with little or no risk.

Most savings accounts carry little or no risk. Take advantage of this by looking for the savings account that offers the best return.

**Tip # 314:** As you get older, transfer more money from stocks to bonds.

As you approach retirement, take your money out of risky stocks and into AAA-rated and government bonds. Your average return will be lower, but you will protect yourself against losing a large chunk of your net worth with just a few years of work to get it back.

**Tip # 315:** Set aside money for savings before allocating money to any other budget category.

Consider saving first and spending later. Intuitively, this may seem like the other way around, but in reality, it's a great habit to develop.

**Tip # 316:** Develop good saving habits.

Get in the habit of putting extra money in your savings whenever you have it, rather than looking for ways to spend it.

# 365 Tip $ for your financial life

**Tip # 317:** Start saving early.

Instead of waiting until your 30s or 40s to start saving for retirement, start saving while you're young. Compound interest will make this investment decision worthwhile.

**Tip # 318:** Get a free savings account.

Instead of getting a savings account that requires multiple fees and payments, look for a free account. In most situations, if you keep at least € 100 in the account, you can do it for free.

**Tip # 319:** Try to negotiate a lower rate in exchange for using direct deposit.

Some banks will give you incentives to use direct deposit and wire transfers, rather than check cashing. See if you can use this as a bargaining chip to negotiate lower rates.

**Tip # 320:** Credit cards that offer rebates or rewards may not always be the best option.

Even if a card offers a 3% cash back, it may not be the best card for you. Consider other dimensions of the card, such as its APR and its annual fee.

**Tip # 321:** Set savings goals.

Decide how much you want to save before you hit your 30s, 40s, and 50s. Set specific goals and try to stick to them.

**Tip # 322:** Execute your savings goals.

When it comes to your savings plan, execution is key. It's one thing to say, "I want to have at least $ 60,000 / year to live on after I retire," and it's another to make it happen. Don't get too carried away when trying to execute your savings plan.

**Tip # 323:** Set goals for your business.

## 365 Tip $ for your financial life

If you own a business, set goals for its growth and development. Instead of letting things drift, force them to move in a favorable direction.

**Tip # 324:** Set personal financial goals.

When it comes to personal finances, stay on track by setting goals. For example, set a goal to create and stick to a monthly budget. Or set a goal not to miss a single bill (or pay late) for an entire year.

**Tip # 325:** Periodically evaluate how well you have kept your goals.

On a regular basis, decide if you've met your business and financial goals. If you are doing it wrong, ask why. And also think about how you can improve.

**Tip # 326:** Be consistent with your saving habits.

Every now and then, we convince ourselves that we don't need to save when our lives get financially difficult. However, in reality, we are preparing to alternate between good and bad saving behaviors.

365 Tip $ for your financial life

**Tip # 327:** Find a better job.

An important way to increase your income is simply to find a better job. If you've been working in the same place for 10 years and have received few raises, consider taking advantage of your experience and switching to a job that is willing to pay you more.

**Tip # 328:** Don't buy things you can't afford.

In general, a good way to save money is to avoid buying things you can't afford. If you can't afford a big screen TV without paying for it with credit, don't buy it.

**Tip # 329:** If you are a student, buy pocket versions of the textbooks.

As a student, textbooks can be incredibly expensive. For this reason, you should try looking for pocket and second-hand versions on half.com, Amazon.com, and other book resellers.

# 365 Tip $ for your financial life

**Tip # 330:** Buy electronic versions of tangible products.

If a product comes in tangible and electronic form, go electronic. It will often be considerably cheaper.

**Tip # 331:** Visit retailmenot.com to get coupons before you pay.

When purchasing items from online retail stores, check retailmenot.com to determine if coupons are available for that store.

**Tip # 332:** Recycle your old clothes into things you need.

If you have old clothes that you don't wear, consider upcycling them into something you need, such as a wall decoration, a wallet, or a bracelet.

**Tip # 333:** Use old decorations in new ways.

## 365 Tip $ for your financial life

A vase with flowers can be turned into a vase with sand or decorative beads. Get creative in using old decorations to make new ones.

**Tip # 334:** Use book exchange websites to get new books.

Use a book exchange site to exchange your old books that you have already read for new ones. This is a great alternative to constantly buying new books.

**Tip # 335:** Use websites that pay you to sign up.

Create an extra email and many websites pay you some money to register. Make all the available ones and use that money to invest, since you did not have it.

**Tip # 336:** Use websites that pay you to bring friends.

They are usually the same as advice 335. Not only do they pay you to register, but they pay you another extra for referred friends.

365 Tip $ for your financial life

**Tip # 337:** Unplug electronics when not in use.

When not in use, many electronic devices still draw power when plugged in. Therefore, from now on, unplug energy-absorbing appliances when not in use.

Tip # 338: Use a power strip with your electronic devices in your entertainment center.

Use one power strip with all electronic devices in your entertainment center. When not in use, turn the power strip off.

**Tip # 339:** Turn off the tap while brushing your teeth.

Saving water can lower your utility bills. So the next time you brush your teeth, remember to turn off the water, instead of letting it run.

**Tip # 340:** Spend less time in the shower.

# 365 Tip $ for your financial life

As with tip 339, try to save water by spending less time in the shower.

**Tip # 341:** Bottle your own water.

Instead of buying expensive bottled water, fill a water bottle from your home tap.

**Tip # 342:** Use rechargeable batteries.

Instead of constantly buying new batteries, buy rechargeable batteries, which will last many cycles.

**Tip # 343:** If you have a young child, use cloth diapers.

If you have a young child, consider using cloth diapers instead of plastic diapers to save costs.

**Tip # 344:** Use the Internet in the library and public spaces.

## 365 Tip $ for your financial life

Instead of paying for an Internet connection at home, use the Internet at the library.

**Tip # 345:** Use public goods and services.

Make use of public goods and services, such as public Wi-Fi stations.

**Tip # 346:** Take advantage of free promotional offers from local businesses.

When companies offer free food and drinks or free promotional productions, take advantage of these offers.

**Tip # 347:** Water your lawn less often.

To save on your utility bills, try to water your lawn less often.

**Tip # 348:** Use powdered juice mixes instead of soda.

# 365 Tip $ for your financial life

Instead of buying bottles of soda, drink tap water mixed with powdered juice. This will be considerably less expensive.

**Tip # 349:** when traveling, stay at a friend's house, rather than a hotel.

If you are planning to go on vacation or visit friends or family, plan to stay at someone's home, rather than a hotel. You could save hundreds on a week-long trip.

**Tip # 350:** Use couchsurfing.com to find places to stay while traveling.

If you have no one to stay with on your next trip, use couchsurfing.com to locate people who are willing to welcome visitors to their homes.

**Tip # 351:** Keep an eye on social networking sites, like Twitter, for limited-time offers.

Many businesses, including retail stores, airlines, and others, offer limited-time deals on Twitter. By taking advantage of these short offers, you can save hundreds of dollars.

# 365 Tip $ for your financial life

**Tip # 352:** Take surveys to get free stuff.

Today, many companies offer free products and cash in exchange for completing surveys. Do this whenever possible.

**Tip # 353:** If you are not satisfied with a product or service, contact the company.

If you are not satisfied with a product or service, you might consider contacting the company that produced it. In many cases, they will be willing to offer a refund or free products.

Tip # 354: Try new product samples before you buy.

Before making a major purchase, try a free sample. For example, drive a car before you buy it. Or try an expensive food or wine before buying large quantities.

**Tip # 355:** Print photos at a local store, rather than using an expensive photo printer.

Instead of buying an expensive photo printer, print your photos at a local print shop. This is generally cheaper than paying for ink for a photo printer.

**Tip # 356:** Use a tdt television, instead of cable.

If you are short on money, ditch the cable and use tdt television. This can save you hundreds over the course of a year.

**Tip # 357:** Contact your TV and Internet provider for the latest packages and offers.

If you think you are paying too much for your TV and Internet, contact your cable company for the latest offers. You may find that similar packages are now available at a much lower price.

**Tip # 358:** Don't let the batteries in your electronic products run down to 0%.

## 365 Tip $ for your financial life

Don't let the batteries in your electronic devices drain completely on a regular basis. This will reduce the overall long-term life of the battery.

**Tip # 359:** Look for used items on Craigslist or eBay.

If you need a new rack or a new tire for your car, check Craigslist and eBay first before you go anywhere else. Not only will you be able to compare prices more easily, but you will also save a lot of money.

**Tip # 360:** When shopping, look for "day before" food that is already on sale.

One-day foods, such as bread, are often sold at a steep discount at the grocery store. Look for this section to get great discounts.

**Tip # 361:** Take your pets to a non-profit vet.

Non-profit vets often offer considerably lower fees. Look for one before you go to vets for profit.

# 365 Tip $ for your financial life

**Tip # 362:** Eat at home. Don't ask outside.

Instead of ordering food, eat at home. This will save you money; and it can even save you time waiting for a delivery.

**Tip # 363:** In the winter, seal your windows with plastic wrap to save money on heating.

Better insulating your home can dramatically lower your energy costs. One way to do this is by covering the windows with plastic.

**Tip # 364:** Just heat or condition the part of the house you are using.

If you're not using a room, don't pay to heat or condition it. Instead, turn off the heater or air conditioner.

**Tip # 365:** Look online for free local forms of entertainment.

## 365 Tip $ for your financial life

Before you spend hundreds of dollars on entertainment, first see if you can find local entertainment through online ad services. In many cases, you will be able to find free events in your area that will give you as much fun as you could get from an expensive night.

## Conclusion

Now you've read 365 tips for living frugally, saving your money, earning more money, and investing your money wisely. Only you know which of these tips can transform your life and which ones are best ignored.

So keep this document close by, choose your advice selectively and wisely; and then follow the tips in the tip once you have decided to follow them. Many of the councils discussed have comprehensive books on the subject. Keep researching and adapt them to your way of life.

When it comes to making good personal financial decisions, a plan is important. But the plan alone won't get you there without clean execution, hard work, and tough decisions.

## 365 Tip $ for your financial life

We tend to take time to make decisions, and once made we change them quickly if we think it is necessary. Financially free people make quick decisions and only if they are convinced of the new landscape do they change them.

And with this, I leave you to grow your wealth, achieve financial security, and be happy with your life and your decisions.